IMPACTING EARTH
HOW PEOPLE CHANGE THE LAND

DIGGING MINES AND WELLS

JASON BRAINARD

PowerKiDS press
New York

Published in 2019 by The Rosen Publishing Group, Inc.
29 East 21st Street, New York, NY 10010

First Edition

Editor: Jennifer Lombardo
Book Design: Tanya Dellaccio

Photo Credits: Cover Tim Roberts Photography/Shutterstock.com; p. 5 Jason Benz Bennee/Shutterstock.com; p. 7 Alexander Loos/EyeEm/Getty Images; p. 9 Anan Kaewkhammul/Shutterstock.com; p. 10 Kuznetcov_Konstantin/Shutterstock.com; p. 11 Sunshine Seeds/Shutterstock.com; pp. 12, 15 Monty Rakusen/Cultura/Getty Images; p. 13 dpa picture alliance/Alamy Stock Photo; p. 17 Visuals Unlimited, Inc./Walt Anderson/Getty Images; p. 19 (both) VCG/Visual China Group/Getty Images; p. 20 Abbin Chittilappilly/Shutterstock.com; p. 21 Bildagentur Zoonar GmbH/Shutterstock.com; p. 22 Nataly Reinch/Shutterstock.com.

Cataloging-in-Publication Data

Names: Brainard, Jason.
Title: Digging mines and wells / Jason Brainard.
Description: New York : PowerKids Press, 2019. | Series: Impacting Earth: how people change the land | Includes glossary and index.
Identifiers: ISBN 9781538341889 (pbk.) | ISBN 9781538341902 (library bound) | ISBN 9781538341896 (6pack)
Subjects: LCSH: Excavating machinery–Juvenile literature. | Earthmoving machinery–Juvenile literature. | Mines and mineral resources--Juvenile literature.
Classification: LCC TA735.B73 2019 | DDC 621.8'65–dc23

Manufactured in the United States of America

CPSIA Compliance Information: Batch #CWPK19. For Further Information contact Rosen Publishing, New York, New York at 1-800-237-9932

CONTENTS

WHY WE DIG

Have you ever wondered how cars run or what makes a phone work? The answer to both these questions begins deep beneath Earth. Many of the things we use every day have to be removed from the ground. This changes the way the land looks. Sometimes this can be bad for our planet.

THE DEEPEST HOLE EVER

The Kola Superdeep Borehole in Russia is more than 7 miles (11.3 km) deep. It took more than 20 years to dig.

OPEN CAST MINE, AUSTRALIA

WHAT IS A MINE?

A mine is a hole dug in the earth to help people reach things they need or want. Mines are very deep and can cause a lot of danger to people's health and safety. Mining can also make the water, air, or land dirty and unsafe. This hurts the earth and the things that live on it.

WHY DO WE NEED MINES?

Gold, iron, and coal all come from mines. There's no other way to get to them.

WHAT IS A WELL?

A well is a hole dug to remove **liquids** and gases from within the earth. Some people use a well to get drinking water from deep in the ground. Other wells reach oil, which is used to make the gasoline that powers our cars. There are also wells for natural gas, which is used to heat buildings.

OIL WELL

JOBS, JOBS, JOBS

People dug the earliest mines using hand tools. Some mines are dug into the sides of mountains. Others are dug as deep holes in the ground. Today, miners have to learn a lot more than miners of the past did. Computers control many mining tools now, so miners have to learn how to use them.

HUMAN AND MACHINE

In the past, people dug mines. Now machines do most of the work.

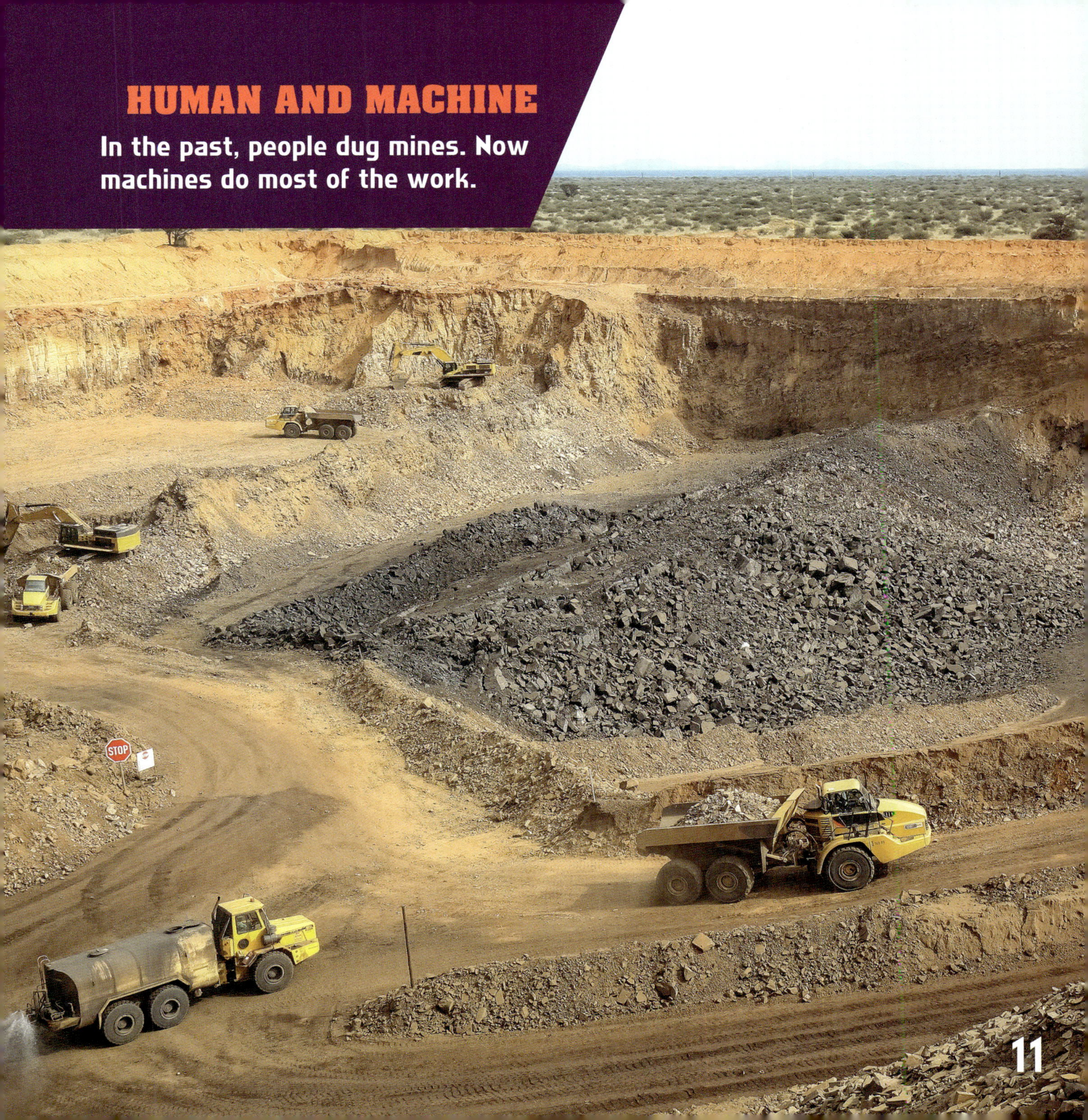

REALLY BIG MACHINES

Modern mining requires some of the biggest machines people have ever made. Giant drills and saws cut into the earth. Excavators are large machines that dig up dirt. Excavators load up huge trucks with the things that come from mines. Large **pumps** are used to remove oil, gas, and water from the ground.

THAT'S BIG!

The Bagger 293 excavator is the world's largest land vehicle. It's about 722 feet (220.1 m) long!

SAFE REMOVAL

Mining can still be full of danger, so miners must be careful. Safety is the most important thing to think about at any mine. Special pumps and **filters** keep the air the miners breathe clean and safe. Without them, dust and gases could start a fire or make the miners sick.

A BIG MESS

Much of the matter left over from mining contains **poisons**. Miners need to put it in special places where it won't get into people's food, water, or air. In the near future, power from the sun and wind may make mining for oil and gas less necessary. That means there will be less waste. This will be better for Earth, as well as people, animals, and plants.

TAILINGS

Tailings are the things left over from mining. They include rocks as well as things that are poisonous to people and animals.

POLLUTED WATER IN A MINE

CLEANING UP

When a mine still has things in it people can use, it is called "productive." A mine stops being productive after we've removed all the **resources** from it. At this point, people may change the land into something else we can use. Sometimes we can turn an old mine into something useful. The Deep Pit Hotel in Shanghai, China, shown here, is one example.

DEEP PIT HOTEL

GOING SHOPPING

So, what do we get for all this work? We use gold to make jewelry. We burn coal to give us **electricity**. Natural gas is used to heat buildings. Oil is needed to make plastic and run cars. Without mines and wells, life would be very different.

COAL MINE

GETTING IT RIGHT

Without mines and wells, we wouldn't have cars, telephones, or even hot water. But our activities change the land in ways that can hurt plants, animals, and people. We can't avoid all the bad things that come with using mines and wells, but if we're careful, we can make them safer than ever before.

GLOSSARY

electricity: A form of energy that is carried through wires and is used to operate machines, lights, etc.

filter: Something that removes harmful things from air or water.

liquid: Something, such as water, that can flow freely.

poison: Something that can make living things sick or kill them.

pump: A machine that moves a gas or a liquid from one place to another.

resource: Something that can be used.

INDEX

WEBSITES

Due to the changing nature of Internet links, PowerKids Press has developed an online list of websites related to the subject of this book. This site is updated regularly. Please use this link to access the list:
www.powerkidslinks.com/hpcl/mines